Pray & Color

30 Days of Thanks and Praise
A Devotional Coloring Journal

By Sonja Sorenson

30 Days of Thanks and Praise
A Devotional Coloring Journal

PRAY & COLOR

[WWW.SINGASONJA.COM]

[SINGASONJA@AOL.COM]

Welcome to Pray and Color- 30 Days of Thanks and Praise. This devotional journal came from a desire to slow down and meditate on the words of God in scripture. It is often a struggle to not be distracted. Coloring provides a restful place for your brain and allows for stress free focus. My suggested use is to read aloud the verse, and then color letting the message sink into your spirit. Allow time to rewrite the verse in your own words as a prayer. It is always amazing to see the new insights as you write them down! If you have another way of using the devotional, I'd love to hear about it. Join the community at our facebook group or my website. I would love to meet you! Sonja

Sonja Sorenson

10/17/2015

All designs are copyrighted. Feel free to copy for your own use if you desire multiple copies and direct your friends to my website page for some freebies!

All scriptures are public domain. King James Version (KJV) by Public Domain or World English Bible (WEB) by Public Domain. The name "World English Bible" is trademarked.

ISBN-13:
978-1517779009

ISBN-10:
1517779006

Psalm 104:33-34 King James Version (KJV)

I will sing unto the LORD as long as I live: I will sing praise to my God while I have my being.

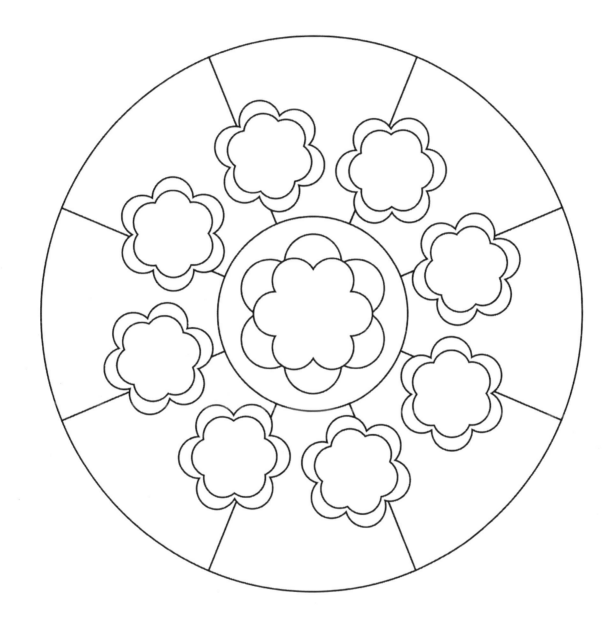

Psalm 24:1 King James Version (KJV)

The earth is the LORD's, and the fullness thereof; the world, and they that dwell therein.

PHILIPPIANS 4:8 KING JAMES VERSION (KJV)

Finally, brethren, whatsoever things are true, whatsoever things are honest, whatsoever things are just, whatsoever things are pure, whatsoever things are lovely, whatsoever things are of good report; if there be any virtue, and if there be any praise, think on these things.

Psalm 119:11 King James Version (KJV)

Thy word have I hid in mine heart, that I might not sin against thee.

Psalm 104:34 King James Version (KJV)

My meditation of him shall be sweet: I will be glad in the LORD.

Psalm 139:13 King James Version (KJV)

For thou hast possessed my reins: thou hast covered me in my mother's womb.

ZEPHANIAH 3:17 KING JAMES VERSION (KJV)

The LORD thy God in the midst of thee is mighty; he will save, he will rejoice over thee with joy; he will rest in his love, he will joy over thee with singing.

John 15:15 King James Version (KJV)

Henceforth I call you not servants; for the servant knoweth not what his lord doeth: but I have called you friends; for all things that I have heard of my Father I have made known unto you.

Psalm 22:4-5 King James Version (KJV)

*O**ur fathers trusted in thee: they trusted, and thou didst deliver them.*
   They cried unto thee, and were delivered: they trusted in thee, and were not confounded.

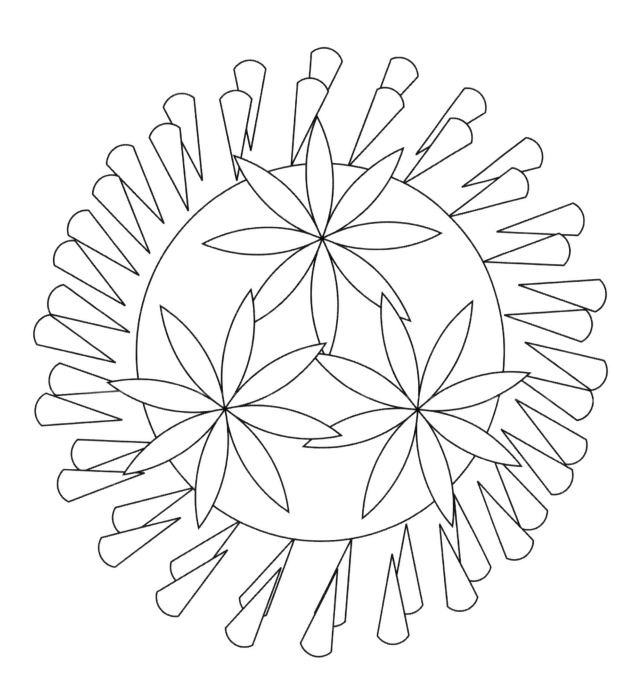

PHILIPPIANS 1:3 KING JAMES VERSION (KJV)

I thank my God upon every remembrance of you,

Colossians 3:15 King James Version (KJV)

And let the peace of God rule in your hearts, to which also ye are called in one body; and be ye thankful.

2 Corinthians 12:9 King James Version (KJV)

And he said unto me, My grace is sufficient for thee: for my strength is made perfect in weakness. Most gladly therefore will I rather glory in my infirmities, that the power of Christ may rest upon me.

Psalm 100:3 King James Version (KJV)

Know ye that the LORD he is God: it is he that hath made us, and not we ourselves; we are his people, and the sheep of his pasture.

Psalm 19:1 King James Version (KJV)

The heavens declare the glory of God; and the firmament sheweth his handiwork.

Psalm 40:5 King James Version (KJV)

Many, O LORD my God, are thy wonderful works which thou hast done... and if I would declare and speak of them, they are more than can be numbered.

PSALM 100:4 WORLD ENGLISH BIBLE (WEB)

*E*nter *into his gates with thanksgiving,* into his courts with praise. Give thanks to him, and bless his name.

Hebrews 13:15 King James Version (KJV)

By him therefore let us offer the sacrifice of praise to God continually, that is, the fruit of our lips giving thanks to his name.

PHILIPPIANS 4:6 WORLD ENGLISH BIBLE (WEB)

In nothing be anxious, but in everything, by prayer and petition with thanksgiving, let your requests be made known to God.

1 Thessalonians 5:18 King James Version (KJV)

In everything give thanks: for this is the will of God in Christ Jesus concerning you.

PHILIPPIANS 4:7 WORLD ENGLISH BIBLE (WEB)

And the peace of God, which surpasses all understanding, will guard your hearts and your thoughts in Christ Jesus.

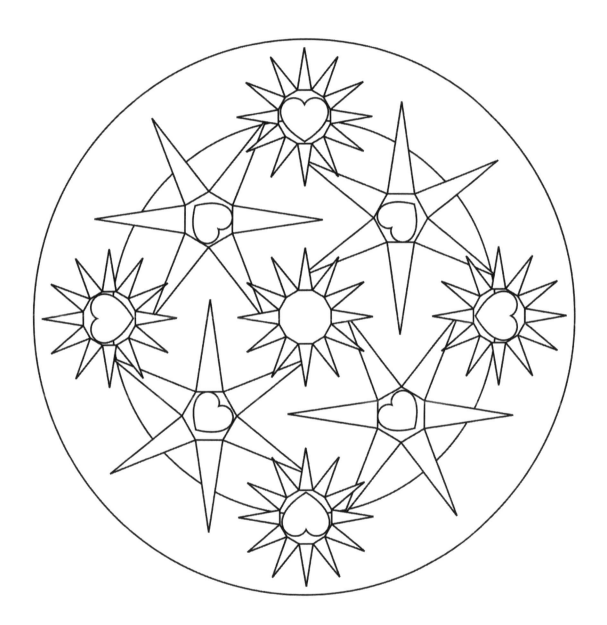

1 Corinthians 15:57 King James Version (KJV)

But thanks be to God, which giveth us the victory through our Lord Jesus Christ.

1 Chronicles 16:8 King James Version (KJV)

Give thanks unto the LORD, call upon his name, make known his deeds among the people.

1 Chronicles 16:34 King James Version (KJV)

O give thanks unto the LORD; for he is good; for his mercy endureth for ever.

Psalm 69:30 King James Version (KJV)

I will praise the name of God with a song, and will magnify him with thanksgiving.

Psalm 75:1 King James Version (KJV)

Unto thee, O God, do we give thanks, unto thee do we give thanks: for that thy name is near thy wondrous works declare.

Psalm 79:13 King James Version (KJV)

So we thy people and sheep of thy pasture will give thee thanks for ever: we will shew forth thy praise to all generations.

Psalm 95:2 King James Version (KJV)

Let us come before his presence with thanksgiving, and make a joyful noise unto him with psalms.

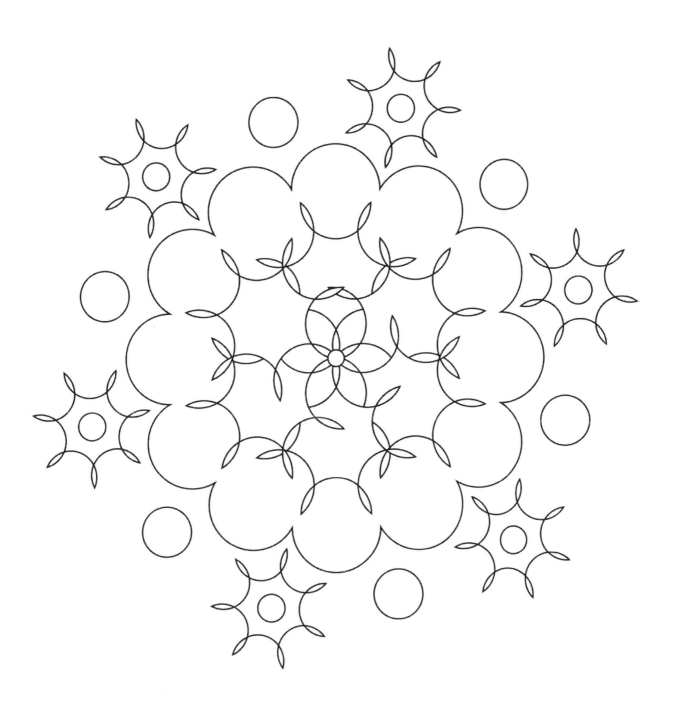

Psalm 97:12 King James Version (KJV)

Rejoice in the LORD, ye righteous; and give thanks at the remembrance of his holiness.

Psalm 100:4 King James Version (KJV)

Enter into his gates with thanksgiving, and into his courts with praise: be thankful unto him, and bless his name.

If you have enjoyed this book, check out some additional pages at www.singasonja.com or join the community at Pray & Color on facebook.

Volume 2 of the Pray & Color series is 30 Days of Rejoicing!

Deuteronomy 12:7 King James Version (KJV)

And there ye shall eat before the LORD your God, and ye shall rejoice in all that ye put your hand unto, ye and your households, wherein the LORD thy God hath blessed thee.

Made in the USA
Middletown, DE
22 February 2016